Th   're the last date shown bel

Cover *United Nations troops enter Sinai at the end of the Suez crisis to safeguard against Israeli reimposition.*

Frontispiece *On 1 November 1956 Nasser ordered some 50 ships to be scuttled in the Suez Canal, in retaliation to an Anglo-French offensive.*

THE SUEZ CRISIS

Paul Harper

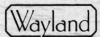

FLASHPOINTS

The Arab–Israeli Issue
The Conflict in Afghanistan
The Cuban Missile Crisis
The Hungarian Uprising
The Irish Question
The Revolution in Iran
The Rise of Solidarity
The Suez Crisis
The Vietnam War

First published in 1986 by
Wayland (Publishers) Ltd
61 Western Road, Hove
East Sussex BN3 1JD, England

© Copyright 1986 Wayland (Publishers) Ltd

Typeset by The Bath Press, Avon
Printed and bound in the UK
at The Bath Press, Avon

British Library Cataloguing in Publication Data
Harper, Paul
    The Suez crisis.——(Flashpoints)
    1. Egypt——History——Intervention, 1956
    I. Title   II. Series
    956'.044   DT107.83

ISBN 0-85078-776-9

Contents

1
From Sinai to Suez

Egypt's Sinai desert in the mid-1950s was a dangerous place: an empty, waterless wilderness of sand dunes and bare mountain rock, virtually devoid of life but for the Egyptian and Israeli military outposts dotted along the two countries' common frontier at the eastern edge of the peninsula. There was no international border, only a disputed armistice line between two nations in a state of war. Sinai was the scene of constant skirmishes and raids under cover of darkness to commit murder and sabotage behind enemy lines.

Israel's surprise attack
On 29 October 1956, conflict in Sinai suddenly escalated into full-scale war as Israel unleashed a surprise attack across the desert towards the heart of Egypt and the strategic Suez Canal. Fast, mobile armoured columns and troops struck out in a three-pronged attack: westwards, toward the Canal, and south, to the peninsula's tip, where Egypt maintained a blockade of the approaches to Israel's port of Eilat in the Gulf of Aqaba.

Most daring of all, Israeli soldiers were parachuted far ahead of the advance to secure Sinai's mountain passes for their forces advancing on the ground. The elite paratroopers suffered heavy losses as the rapidly mobilising Egyptian army laid ambushes among the narrow mountain passes that guarded the way to the Canal. Israel explained its lightning assault to the world as an attempt to destroy the bases from which Arab guerillas had been mounting attacks on Israel. But it was far more than that.

The day after the attack began, the governments of France and Britain delivered a joint ultimatum to Egypt and Israel, demanding that they withdraw their forces from the proximity of the Canal as the fighting between them threatened 'to disrupt the freedom of navigation through the Suez Canal on which the economic life of many nations depends.' If

Opposite The map indicates the direction of Israel's surprise attack on Egypt, along with the Anglo–French landings some days later.

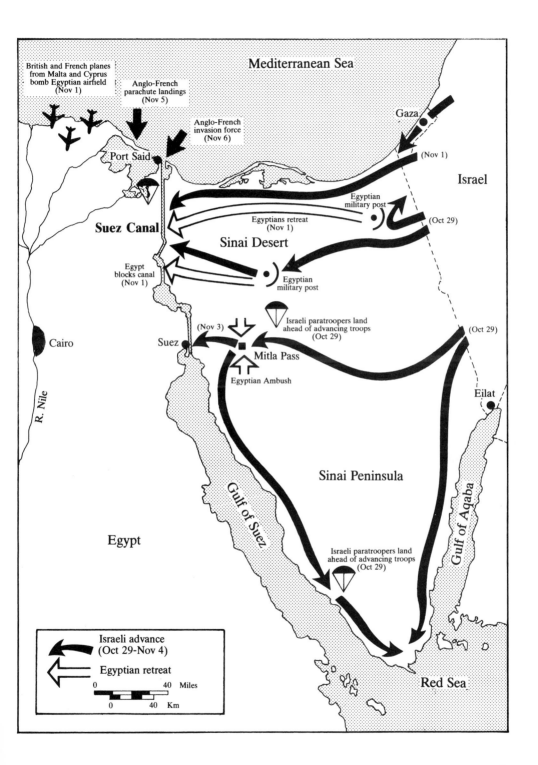

British and French planes from Malta and Cyprus bomb Egyptian airfield (Nov 1)

Anglo-French parachute landings (Nov 5)

Anglo-French invasion force (Nov 6)

Mediterranean Sea

Port Said

Gaza

Israel

(Nov 1)

Egyptian military post

(Oct 29)

Suez Canal

Egyptians retreat (Nov 1)

Sinai Desert

Egypt blocks canal (Nov 1)

Egyptian military post

(Oct 29)

Cairo

Israeli paratroopers land ahead of advancing troops (Oct 29)

Suez

(Nov 3)

Mitla Pass

Egyptian Ambush

Eilat

R. Nile

Sinai Peninsula

Gulf of Suez

Gulf of Aqaba

Egypt

Israeli paratroopers land ahead of advancing troops (Oct 29)

Red Sea

Israeli advance (Oct 29-Nov 4)

Egyptian retreat

0   40 Miles

0   40 Km

9

Above 1 November:
Israeli armoured
divisions during their
offensive in Sinai.

they did not stop fighting and withdraw within 12 hours, British and French forces would 'intervene in whatever strength may be necessary to secure compliance'.

Britain and France in collusion

The ultimatum was confirmation for many that Israel's invasion had been planned beforehand in collusion with Britain and France—planned to provide an excuse for striking a decisive blow against Egypt's radical leader, Gamal Abd an-Nasser. Nasser's championship of Arab 'nationalism' and defiance of the Western powers had interfered with American and Western European plans for the region. Previous planning of the event was also confirmed by the fact that, when the British and French ultimatum was issued, Israel's forces were still far from reaching the 10-mile exclusion zone around the Canal called for in the ultimatum. Thus in effect, Israel was being invited to occupy a large stretch of Egyptian territory that its forces had not yet conquered, while Egypt was to abandon all of its Sinai peninsula to the enemy without a fight. Israel immediately accepted the terms; Nasser naturally refused.

Above *British Prime Minister, Anthony Eden, and French Foreign ministers meet to discuss a joint Suez policy before the crisis.*

Left *Colonel Gamal Abd an-Nasser in 1952. He refused to comply with the joint ultimatum issued by Britain and France during the crisis, sensing collusion between the two countries.*

On 1 November, British and French planes flying from bases in Malta and Cyprus began bombing Egyptian airfields, destroying in 48 hours most of Egypt's Soviet-supplied airforce on the ground. Israel's serious fear in invading Sinai had been that Egypt might retaliate by bombing Israeli cities. With Egypt's airforce destroyed, this was no longer a worry.

France and Britain's pretence that they were acting as 'international policemen', halting a dangerous war and safeguarding the Canal for world shipping, was rapidly becoming too absurd to be maintained. It was now that Nasser gave the order for some 50 ships to be scuttled in the shallow waters of the Canal, blocking it completely to traffic. Fearing also that Israel's Sinai attack was a ploy to trap the Egyptian army in the peninsula and leave the country defenceless before an Anglo–French attack, he withdrew all the forces he could west of the Canal.

To all intents and purposes, the fighting between Israeli and Egyptian forces ended, and far from safeguarding the Canal, the menacing posture of Britain and France had led to its closure. Yet the vast Anglo–French invasion fleet that had set sail from Algiers and Malta when the ultimatum expired still kept to its course on the six-day voyage to Egypt.

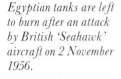

Egyptian tanks are left to burn after an attack by British 'Seahawk' aircraft on 2 November 1956.

In the words of Anthony Nutting, Britain's Foreign Office minister who resigned in protest at his government's action, 'we were to take part in a cynical act of aggression, dressing ourselves for the part as firemen or policemen, while making sure that our fire-hoses spouted petrol and not water and that we belaboured with our truncheons the assaulted and not the assaulter'.

A view of the canal after Nasser's orders to scuttle over 50 ships harboured there.

UN calls for ceasefire

Outraged opposition, both at home and abroad, mounted against the governments of France and Britain. Already the two countries had for the first time used their vetoes in the United Nations Security Council against a resolution, (submitted by their closest ally the United States), calling on Israel to withdraw its forces. On 2 November the UN's General Assembly voted 64–5 for a US-sponsored resolution calling for a ceasefire. This resolution, backed by the largest majority ever received in the Assembly, was immediately accepted by Egypt. Only intense British and French pressure on Israel prevented it from also accepting—for this would have ruined the illusion that Anglo–French forces were attempting to restore peace in the region.

All hostilities between Israel and Egypt had indeed ceased when on 5 November, condemned and isolated by virtually the entire world, Britain and France dropped between them over 1000 paratroopers in and around Port Said, at the northern mouth of the Canal. The violence that had so recently subsided flared again. Arms had been distributed to Egypt's civilian population on the orders of Nasser, round whom his

Opposite Suez *headlines from Britain's leading national newspapers on 31 October 1956.*

Below As the USSR *and the USA vote in favour of the UN ceasefire plan in Egypt, Britain uses its veto for the first time.*

15

Above British
paratroopers in Cyprus,
embarking on their Suez
mission.

supporters now rallied with an enthusiasm brought to fever
pitch by their leader's dramatic stand against the hated 'Western imperialists'. The Suez affair rapidly assumed all the pro-
portions of a full-scale international crisis. The Soviet Union
gratefully seized on the chance to divert attention from its
own bloody invasion of Hungary which was raging simul-
taneously. It threatened to send Russian volunteers to Egypt
to 'crush the aggressors', and Soviet Premier, Bulganin, also

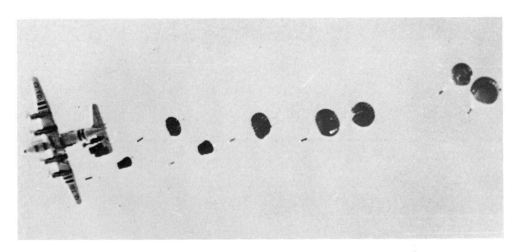

dropped sinister hints to France and Britain about the power of the USSR's nuclear-armed missiles. The next day the guns of the 200 French and British warships standing off Port Said fired off a devastating bombardment before landing 22,000 troops, many by the then novel use of helicopters. The Egyptians defended their now badly damaged city fiercely but were quickly overwhelmed, and the invaders turned south to advance down the Canal.

Above *The British airbourne assault on El Gamil airfield near Port Said.*

'A political storm'

Although finding little military resistance from Egypt, the political storm that France and Britain were now courting was immense. Added to the anger and opposition of the US and the international community at large, Britain's Conservative Government was being affected by an economic crisis that threatened to grind the country to a halt. More senior officials resigned and even the most loyal sections of the press were openly critical, as an already low pound fell further in value. Britain was financially dependent on Middle East oil, the flow of which had been stopped by the closure of the Canal and retaliatory action by other Arab states. It could only keep its industry functioning by importing oil from American sources, the purchase of which was impossible without a massive loan from the US. This, America would do only on condition of a ceasefire and withdrawal from Egypt. The British Prime Minister, Anthony Eden, finally caved in to the immense pressures from all sides and persuaded France also to agree to a ceasefire, which was announced on 7 November.

British soldiers searching Egyptian Arabs for arms during the crisis.

Less than 18 hours after the landing of the main body of the invasion force, it was all over but for the public condemnation. Under a UN-supervised arrangement British and French forces withdrew over a six-week period. In the case of Israel only the most intense pressure applied by the USA, including the threat of sanctions, finally induced it to withdraw without territorial gain six months later.

Having raised the international temperature to boiling point, provoked the hostility of the entire Third World, and alienated almost every friend and ally, the governments of France and Britain in the end made a humiliating withdrawal, their Middle East plans and policies in ruins. They had achieved the exact opposite of everything they had intended.

After the crisis crowds gathered in Cairo to denounce the Anglo–French invasion.

2
Egypt: a vital gateway

The map shows the distance travelled when using the Suez Canal as compared to sailing around the Cape of Good Hope.

How Britain and France, two of the world's leading powers, whose policies were supposedly guided by sophisticated, democratic processes, came to join in such a misconceived adventure—the invasion of a struggling Third World nation—is a story that can be traced far back into history. The modern armies that invaded Egypt in 1956 were following in the footsteps of countless others, from Alexander the Great to Napoleon Bonaparte. Egypt, a world crossroads where the routes joining Asia, Africa, Europe and the Far East all meet, has always been a glittering prize for those with empires to build. For almost 2,500 years, from 525 BC when the Persians invaded Egypt, until 1952 when Colonel Nasser took power, the country had been ruled by foreigners, military conquerors and their descendants. However,

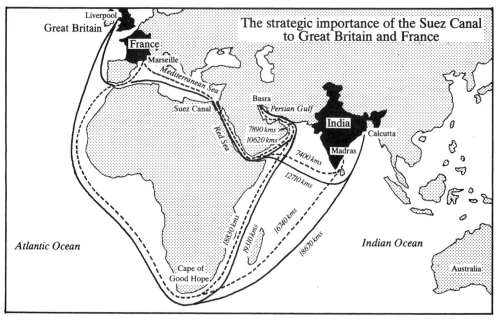

Muhammad Ali, ruler of Egypt from 1805 to 1848, encouraged Egypt's development and independence.

Egyptians have always retained their own distinctive national characteristics, having been Arab in language and culture, and mostly Muslim in faith, since the Arab Conquests of the seventh century AD.

Egypt's strategic importance did not diminish with the rise of the modern sea-based European empires; quite the contrary. For Britain especially, Egypt became the vital gateway to India. It was chiefly for this reason that France, Britain's main rival for world domination in the colonial age, invaded Egypt in 1798. However, Napoleon did not only seek a strategic military conquest, but also a scientific and 'civilizing' mission. He transported with his army a vast number of experts in all fields of knowledge. Though forced out just three years later by a joint operation mounted by Britain and Egypt's nominal sovereign ruler, Napoleon had sowed the seeds of the Arab 'awakening'. A cultural and nationalistic renaissance began, sparked by contact with the West.

The Arab 'awakening'
Muhammad Ali, ruler of Egypt from 1805 to 1848, was very impressed with Europe's technical superiority. His first step towards Egypt's development was to create a

21

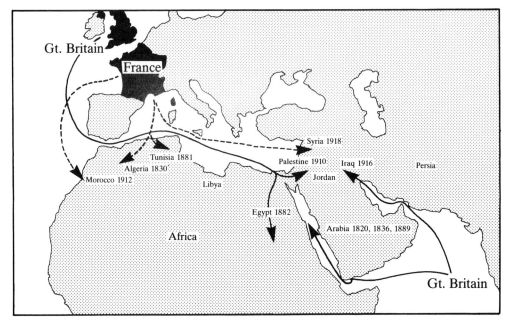

Gt. Britain

France

Syria 1918

Tunisia 1881
Algeria 1830'
Morocco 1912
Libya
Palestine 1910
Jordan
Iraq 1916
Persia

Egypt 1882

Africa
Arabia 1820, 1836, 1889

Gt. Britain

This map shows the extent of Anglo–French imperialism in North Africa.

disciplined army on the Western model, followed by an economic and administrative apparatus to carry out the reforms needed to enable Egypt to enter the new era as his independent domain. State education was introduced, and students were sent to study in Europe, opening for the first time a channel for the communication of Western ideas. Muhammad Ali founded a dynasty that ruled Egypt until Nasser's day, his descendants acquiring formally the title of *Khedive*.

The building of a canal

Anglo–French rivalry in the region continued, as France snapped up most of Arab North Africa for colonies, and both countries competed for a stake in Egypt's future by participating in its development and modernisation under Muhammad Ali's sons and grandsons. French influence finally won.

In a decisive stroke in 1854, Egypt granted a French entrepreneur, Ferdinand de Lesseps, a concession to build a canal across the Suez isthmus to link the Mediterranean and Red Seas, a project first conceived as long ago as the Arab Conquests. It took 15 years and cost the lives of many thousands of Egyptian labourers, conscripted to build the 101-mile waterway deep and wide enough for ocean-going vessels. On 17

November 1869, at an extravagant ceremony attended by many of Europe's ruling monarchs, the Suez Canal was formally opened and the continent of Africa proclaimed a man-made island.

The Canal tied Egypt's fate inextricably with that of the British Empire by rendering obsolete the long, dangerous voyage round the southern Cape of Africa from Britain to its territories in India and the Far East. Within a decade, 70 per cent of the ships passing through it were British. The Canal had become a British imperial lifeline and London's direct control of it was essential if Britain was to remain a world power.

A view of the Suez Canal showing the statue of Ferdinand de Lesseps—the entrepreneur behind the canal project. During the crisis this statue was destroyed by the Egyptians.

The reign of Khedive Ismail, grandson of Muhammad Ali, from 1867 to 1879, was for Egypt a period of rapid and seemingly glorious development, crowned by the triumph of the Canal. Yet all the while the Khedive was borrowing heavily from the West to finance projects. Behind the facade of Westernization, Egypt was being plunged into bankruptcy and the vast majority of Egyptians, their crushing poverty untouched by the changes taking place, were increasingly resentful of what they saw as the arrogant exploitation of their country's resources for the benefit of foreigners and a tiny ruling elite. In 1875 Britain's Prime Minister, Benjamin Disraeli, made use of Egypt's indebted-

ness under Khedive Tawfiq (Ismail's successor), by buying Egypt's 44 per cent share in the Suez Canal Company. Egypt became a virtual European protectorate, as France and Britain took control of the Egyptian economy, which was collapsing completely.

The battle of Tel al-Kabir

In such a setting, an 'Egypt for the Egyptians' movement, inspired by an Egyptian army officer, Colonel Ahmad Arabi, quickly gathered support from all classes of Egyptians: it was directed as much against the Khedive as against foreign domination. In 1882, alarmed by the growing strength of the nationalists, Britain and France sent a joint naval force to Alexandria, where most Europeans in Egypt lived, as a show of force. After riots broke out there, British ships bombarded the city for ten hours. A force then sailed up the Suez Canal and defeated an army hastily assembled by Arabi at the battle of Tel al-Kabir, killing 10,000 Egyptians for the loss of less than 100 British soldiers. Arabi was exiled, and the Khedive confirmed in power as a British puppet.

Thus began Britain's 75-year-long occupation of Egypt. Thereafter Egypt, but above all the Suez Canal, was a reluctant but essential part of Britain's global power and prestige.

Left Cairo 1920: Egyptians have always retained their distinctive national character. From this background an 'Egypt for the Egyptians' movement developed in the late nineteenth century.

25

3
Arab nationalism emerges

By the beginning of the twentieth century, after four centuries as the supreme authority over the Arab and Islamic lands, the old Turkish Ottoman Empire was struggling to survive in the new, Western-dominated age. In London and Paris the great foreign policy debate was the 'Eastern Question'. What would emerge in the place of the Ottoman Empire when it did finally fall? How could its territories be satisfactorily shared out among such intense rivals? The issue was brought

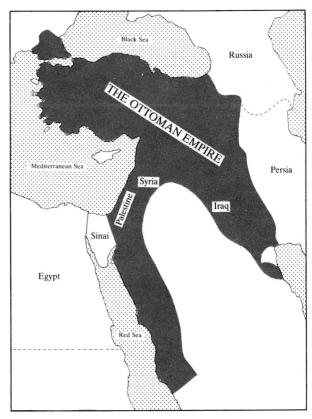

The shaded area shows the extent of the Ottoman Empire until the early twentieth century.

to a head by the outbreak of the First World War in 1914, when Britain, France and Russia found themselves on the same side against Germany and the Turks. The defeat of the Turks in the Middle East would leave the Allies physically in control of those Arab provinces of the Turkish Empire that were not already, like Egypt and North Africa, in their hands.

1917: Arab troops during a campaign in North Africa. In the First World War, Britain promised the Arab nations their independence if they fought against the Ottoman Turks. After the war this promise was short-lived.

The Sykes–Picot Agreement

Anticipating their victory, the Allies in May 1916 concluded a secret pact, the Sykes-Picot Agreement, which divided most of the region between France and Britain, leaving only the sparsely-populated desert areas to be granted to the Arabs themselves.

The Bolshevik Revolution of November 1917 and the entry of the United States into the war prevented the Sykes–Picot Agreement from being implemented exactly as planned. The influence of the anti-colonialist Americans in particular was instrumental in moderating the European occupation of Arab lands under the Mandate system devised by the League of Nations in the post-war years. This gave France and Britain the responsibility of preparing their allotted areas for eventual self-government and independence. In what are today the Arab states of Iraq and Jordan, Britain got around this awkward stipulation by setting up 'puppet' Arab monarchies which gave the illusion of self-rule while allowing virtually total control from London.

27

For the Arabs, all this was a betrayal of the worst order. In 1916 they had been promised their independence by Britain in return for rebelling against their Ottoman rulers and fighting alongside the British against the Turks. For their vital help in winning the war, they now found they had only exchanged one set of foreign rulers for another. Sykes–Picot laid the foundations of Arab mistrust and resentment of the West that is still present today, but nowhere was the political poison longer-lasting or more deadly than in one small Arab province—Palestine, the Holy Land.

Palestine: sowing the seeds of conflict

In 1917, Britain's Foreign Secretary, Lord Balfour, pledged that, 'His Majesty's Government view with favour the establishment in Palestine of a National Home for the Jewish people, and will use their best endeavours to facilitate the achievement of this object ...' Britain conquered Palestine from the Turks the same year, and acquired the Mandate for the country from the League of Nations in 1920. Large-scale Jewish immigration from Europe followed, and Britain seemed unaware or indifferent to the fact that by encouraging the creation of a Jewish state in Palestine, it was also discarding the national

Jewish immigrants making their home in Palestine.

Under leaders such as Saad Zaghloul (above) and Mustafa Kamel (inset) nationalist feeling developed in Egypt.

rights of its Arab inhabitants, 90 per cent of the population in 1918. In this process the seeds of a terrible conflict were sown.

Nationalist ideology develops

Since Colonel Arabi's uprising in 1882, Egypt had become the main sorting-house for the development of nationalist ideas in the Middle East. The father-figures of the Arab

30

nationalist movement, men like Jamal al-Din al-Afghani, Muhammad Abduh, Rashid Rida and Abd al-Rahman al-Kawakibi, all chose Egypt, the intellectual heart of the Arab world and a relative haven from Ottoman repression, as the platform to air their revolutionary ideas. This provoked in the British authorities reactions ranging from contemptuous tolerance to active suppression. The themes of the early nationalists were of reviving, reforming and uniting the Islamic world as a whole, rather than just the Arabs, to counter Western domination.

Local nationalism found leaders in men like Mustafa Kamel (1874–1908) and Saad Zaghloul (1857–1927), later Prime Minister of Egypt. Immediately the First World War ended, Zaghloul formed a delegation (*Wafd* in Arabic) and demanded of Britain the right to present Egypt's case for independence in London, and also at the international Peace Conference in Paris. Britain's refusal was followed by a violent uprising, the 1919 Revolution. After twice deporting Zaghloul, Britain finally realized that there was no-one else of sufficient authority with whom to negotiate Britain's future role in Egypt. In 1922 Britain issued a declaration

Close ties between Britain and Egypt remained during the Second World War. **Below** *Anthony Eden inspecting a section of the Arab Legion.*

31

formally recognising Egypt as a sovereign independent nation, though the British army remained in occupation and the British High Commission kept control of the most important aspects of Egyptian affairs. Elections were held soon after which swept to power Zaghloul's supporters, now organised in a parliamentary party which kept the name of Wafd.

Britain, the Wafd and the Monarchy

Egypt between the wars was a three-way power game between Britain, the Wafd and the Egyptian monarchy now headed by King Farouk. Britain however, always had the advantage of military might. By 1936, Britain and the Wafd nationalists were sufficiently resigned to each other's continued presence to conclude an Anglo–Egyptian treaty. This took the country another stage towards independence, while confirming the role of British forces in the defence of Egypt—especially their right to be stationed in the Canal Zone. When the Second World War broke out, Britain called upon the treaty to resume full military occupation of the country. In 1942, when Germany's

Left The Egyptian Royal Family, headed by King Farouk and Queen Narriman before their exile in 1953.

1941: British forces patrolling the fortifications laid in Egypt to safeguard against General Rommel's advance.

H.M.S. Indefatigable, *one of Britain's largest aircraft carriers of the Second World War, passes through the Suez Canal on her way to joining the Eastern fleet.*

General Rommel was advancing across the desert towards Cairo, the suspected pro-Axis sympathies of King Farouk prompted the British to surround his Royal Palace with tanks, and present the Egyptian head of state with the choice of abdicating, or of appointing a government that would support and co–operate with the Allies. Despite his unpopularity among the Egyptians at large, the humiliation of Farouk's forced submission to the British wounded the pride of the whole nation, and irreversibly damaged Anglo–Egyptian relations. It also inspired a young lieutenant in the Egyptian army, Gamal Abd an-Nasser, to lay his plans for a Free Officers movement with the aim of overthrowing the monarchy and the ineffectual parliament as the first steps towards total liberation from British rule.

4
Nasser's non-alignment

The Second World War proved to be as influential on the balance of power in the Middle East as the First World War. With the demise of the Ottoman Empire and subsequently European imperialism, the region now entered an era of superpower rivalry between America and the Soviet Union. Britain and France conceded their global empires with extreme reluctance, and nowhere more so than in the Middle East.

One area where Britain was keen to end its direct involvement, however, was Palestine. Having introduced and supported the Zionist movement which founded the Jewish state, Britain now found itself trapped by its own conflicting promises to the rebellious Arab majority on one hand and the militant Jewish settlers and immigrants on the other. The latter had grown confident enough of its militia's strength to contest control of the land by force with the native Palestinians, and the infant armies of the neighbouring Arab states too, if necessary.

Britain relinquishes Palestine Mandate

Under strong pressure from the US, Britain turned its dilemma over to the United Nations, which in 1947, to the dismay of the Arabs, ruled in favour of splitting the country in two—an Arab and a Jewish state. Even before Britain pulled out its forces, Zionist militia were attacking Arab towns and villages, driving out as much of the population as possible. On 15 May 1948, the day Britain formally abandoned its Mandate, the Zionists proclaimed the State of Israel. In response, the Arabs attacked and during the bitter war that followed, the ill-prepared Arab armies were easily defeated. Eighty per cent of Palestine was captured and incorporated into the new State of Israel. 800,000 Palestinians, over half of the Arab population, were forced out, or fled never to return. The presence of this vast army of destitute refugees, sheltering

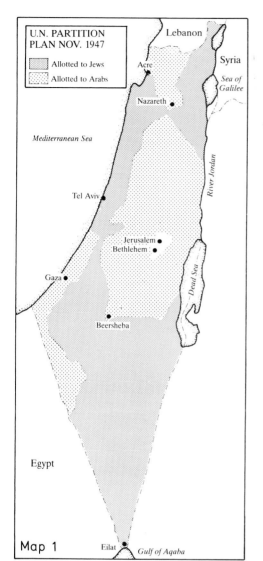

U.N. PARTITION PLAN NOV. 1947

- ▓ Allotted to Jews
- ░ Allotted to Arabs

Lebanon

Acre

Syria

Sea of Galilee

Nazareth

Mediterranean Sea

River Jordan

Tel Aviv

Jerusalem
Bethlehem

Gaza

Dead Sea

Beersheba

Egypt

Map 1

Eilat

Gulf of Aqaba

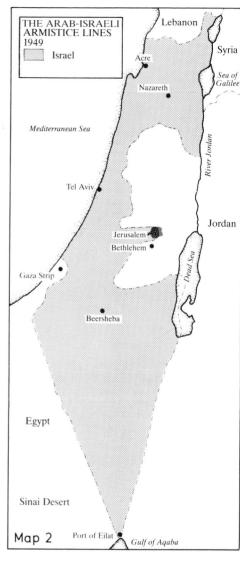

THE ARAB-ISRAELI ARMISTICE LINES 1949

- ▓ Israel

Lebanon

Acre

Syria

Sea of Galilee

Nazareth

Mediterranean Sea

River Jordan

Tel Aviv

Jerusalem
Bethlehem

Jordan

Gaza Strip

Dead Sea

Beersheba

Egypt

Sinai Desert

Map 2

Port of Eilat

Gulf of Aqaba

Map 1 Land allotted in the UN partition plan.
Map 2 The 1948 war led Israel to seize a larger area of land than the UN proposed. As a result, many Palestinians were made homeless.

in the surrounding Arab countries remained ever after both a catalyst for future violence and a reminder to the Arabs of their humiliating defeat.

A wave of anger and revolt swept through the Arab peoples, directed not just at the Western world who, in their eyes, had implanted Israel in their midst, but at their own national leaders for presiding over such a disaster. Nowhere was the backlash stronger than in Egypt, where popular opinion, despite Britain's post-war concession of confining its forces

36

to the Canal Zone, was mounting angrily against the presence of an alien power regarded not only as responsible for the catastrophe in Palestine, but as the main obstacle to true independence. To try and control the political dissent and anti-British riots, the Wafd Government in October 1951 repealed the 1936 Anglo–Egyptian Treaty and began to support sabotage and guerilla attacks against the 80,000 British troops stationed in the Canal Zone. A bloody clash between British soldiers and Egyptian police in January 1952 sparked anti-British riots in Cairo resulting in many deaths and the burning of a large part of the city centre, especially those institutions associated with the British. The descent into anarchy led Nasser's Free Officers movement

Although the Anglo–Egyptian Treaty of 1936 had brought Egypt some way towards self-rule, Britain still remained the obstacle to true independence. In 1952 anti-British riots broke out in Cairo, and many British properties were attacked.
Left *The remains of the British Air Force canteen.*

37

to seize power in an almost bloodless coup six months later, on 23 July. King Farouk was exiled.

Nasser introduces Arab socialism

Like his rebel predecessor of the previous century, Ahmad Arabi, Nasser sprang from the same background of the army, the earliest national institution to be set up by the founder of modern Egypt, Muhammad Ali. And like Arabi, he was a man of the people, with his roots among the *fellahin*, or Egyptian peasants. Though the chief architect of the 1952 coup, Nasser backed away from the limelight of national leadership for almost two years. He did not wait, however, to start implementing his long-planned programmes to

A peasant farming outside Cairo. Nasser was a popular leader, particularly among the Egyptian peasants, for he himself was descended from the fellahin. He quickly instigated a more democratic distribution of the land.

Opposite *As many as 800,000 Palestinians were forced to leave their homeland in 1948, to become refugees in surrounding countries. The destruction of the Jewish quarters in Cairo by Egyptians indicates the sense of outrage felt by the Arab community at large towards the Israelis.*

39

Nasser (sitting, left) and members of the Free Officers Movement who seized power in Egypt in July 1952.

distribute Egypt's land and wealth more fairly—what came to be known as Arab socialism. He also set about eliminating all possible rivals for power among the old Wafd party, which was banned, and the Muslim Brotherhood, a new militant group of Islamic fundamentalists.

The British government took an immediate dislike to Nasser, whom they both feared and mistrusted. At the root of its attitude lay an imperial outlook that had outlived its actual basis, for post-war Britain was a mere shadow of its former imperial grandeur. Yet British politicians of both the left and the right clung stubbornly to the feeling that Egypt was a vital strategic base never to be surrendered. The fact that the empire Egypt was designed to maintain no longer existed (India had become independent in 1947) was not considered.

Nasser's overriding ambition was to expel finally the British presence from Egypt; in addition, his foreign policy of non-alignment with either superpower, and his plans to weld the Arab world in a neutral bloc under Egyptian leadership, were seen by Britain as a direct challenge to its own plans to involve the Arab countries in a Western-sponsored pact. This in itself was part of a wider American scheme to blanket the southern borders of the USSR with a chain of anti-Soviet alliances. American policy at the time, however, appreciating that the Arabs' prime concern was not with the Soviet Union but with Israel, avoided trying to recruit the Arabs into their anti-Communist league.

Nasser's opposition to the British-sponsored Baghdad Pact of 1955 (see glossary), became another bone of contention between Britain and the Arab nationalists, as each tried to encourage the other Arab states to join their respective camps. But Britain was fighting a losing battle. Its influence in the region, once paramount, was anyway waning fast, but to British policy-makers it seemed that it was Nasser who was masterminding every setback the Pact suffered, by orchestrating anti-British propaganda.

Britain's severe criticism of Nasser, was indeed surpassed by the French, who were experiencing a similar process of imperial decay. It was a process made all the worse by the

Arab League members, Nasser, Prince Feisal of Saudi Arabia and Prime Minister of the Yemen, meet for talks in 1955. The League of independent Arab States was formed in 1945 to further cultural, economic, military, political and social co-operation.

41

FLN (Algerian National Liberation Front) members being rounded up by French soldiers. France was convinced that Nasser helped supply arms to these guerillas.

fact that, unlike Britain, France had densely colonised its North African Arab territories: a million French people lived in Algeria, which erupted into nationalist revolt in November 1954. In the long, vicious years of Franco–Algerian fighting that followed, France became convinced, wrongly, that Nasser was the principal inspiration and arms-supplier behind the guerillas of the Front de Libération Nationale (FLN). French governments of varying political hues came to share the belief that any measures were justified against Nasser, 'the Mussolini of the Arab world'.

The Franco–Israeli alliance

To this end France was prepared to go further than Britain, which had to compare any steps taken against Nasser, with the potential effect on relations with the other Arab states over which it still held some influence, in particular Jordan and Iraq. France had less to lose. Its all-out war against Arab nationalism began with the foundation of a close military alliance with Israel, the Arabs' prime enemy. Thus, Israel's military superiority over the Arab states was maintained with a steady flow of sophisticated French weapons. So close was the partnership that it proved but a short step to transform it into outright collusion in a war to topple Nasser from power.

The Franco–Israeli alliance was confirmation for the Arabs that the Jewish state was a Western creation designed not as a haven for a persecuted, homeless people but as a safeguard behind the imperialist retreat from the region— a strategic enemy fortress for the perpetuation of foreign control. In fact Israel had its own, quite different reasons for joining the anti-Nasser front. Under its elder statesman, David Ben Gurion, Israel was actively seeking to test the Egyptian 'superpower' of the Arab world, the most populous and developed Arab state and the one with the greatest potential to decide either for war or peace with Israel.

In the first few years after the Free Officers coup, Egypt's new regime carefully avoided militancy abroad, concentrating public attention and resources instead on internal reform and development. But causes of friction were never far away; in

Israel's David Ben Gurion (left) discusses military plans with General Moshe Dayan during the Suez Crisis.

43

Top and bottom The semi-barren Gaza strip became the home for many Palestinian refugees. The defence of this land proved to be an important issue leading up to the crisis.

particular Egypt's wartime blockade against Israeli shipping in the Gulf of Aqaba, the Suez Canal, and the explosive situation in the Gaza Strip, the tiny, semi-desert wedge of Palestine on the Mediterranean defended and retained by Egyptian forces in the 1948 war. Into this eight by forty kilometre enclave were crammed over 300,000 angry, frustrated Palestinian refugees in conditions of the utmost squalor and poverty. Some took to crossing the barbed wire to their former lands, now occupied by Israeli settlers, either to try and retrieve their property or to take revenge on the new owners. In February 1955, Israeli paratroopers repaid Egypt by attacking their military outpost in Gaza and killing 39 soldiers. In so doing, Israel lit the fuse for the Suez explosion.

44

5
The Crisis erupts

The Israeli raid on Gaza was a profound turning point for Nasser. He had visited the Egyptian soldiers stationed there just before they were attacked and told them that there was nothing to fear, there would be no war. Now many of them had been killed in their sleep, and Gaza was being ransacked by rioting Palestinians demanding arms. The result was to instill in Nasser a deeply-felt obligation to acquire the means for Egypt to defend itself, and most importantly to be able to confront Israel as an equal.

Before Gaza, he had rigorously suppressed the emergence of an armed Palestinian movement in order to avoid Egypt being dragged into a war with Israel which he knew Egypt could not win. But now, to defuse the popular outrage over what was viewed as Israeli provocation, he began to allow Palestinian guerillas to mount raids into Israel from Egyptian territory. From the most peaceful of Israel's frontiers, the Egyptian–Israeli armistice lines degenerated totally, with savage Israeli reprisals following every Palestinian infiltration. Egyptian and Israeli border troops regularly exchanged fire, despite the presence of UN observers intended to uphold the armistice. Nasser knew, however, that Egypt could hold its own only by obtaining a modern arsenal to counter-balance the huge stock of latest weaponry held by Israel.

Nasser appeals to the US for arms
Knowing that Britain and France would not help in building up Egyptian military power, Nasser turned to the United States. President Eisenhower had shown himself to be opposed to the colonialist attitudes of Britain and France in the Middle East, and believed an even-handed stance on the Arab–Israeli conflict was the best way to secure US interests in the region. But his actions had to take into account the considerable power wielded at home by the pro–Israeli Jewish lobby against America's highly profitable oil dealings with the Arab Gulf states,

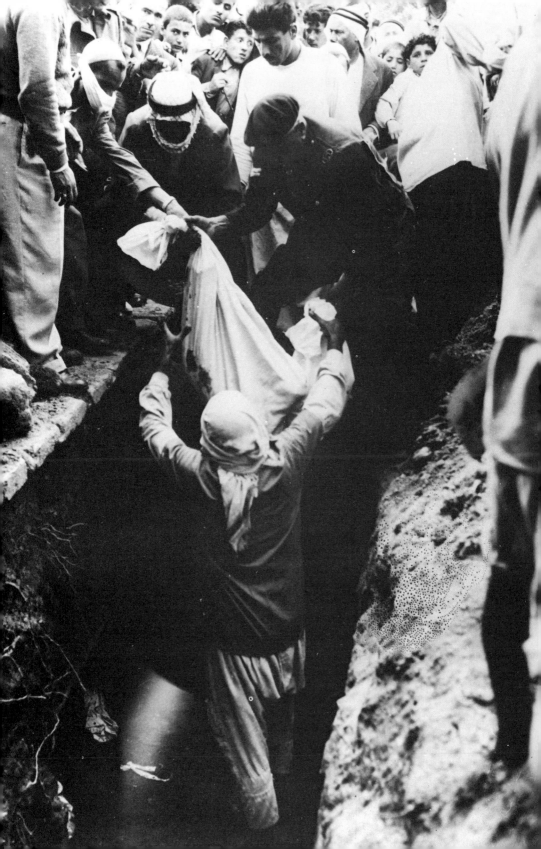

especially Saudi Arabia. It was such considerations that brought about the Tripartite Declaration of 1950, in which the US, Britain and France pledged themselves to take action against any attempt by either Israel or the Arabs to use force to alter the armistice lines, or the military balance of power, resulting from the 1948 war. America did not share the intense Anglo–French antagonism toward Nasser, and it strongly supported moves to get a total withdrawal of British troops from Egypt, which was finally brought about after protracted Anglo–Egyptian negotiations on 31 March 1956.

Nasser's requests to Washington for arms, though modest in scope ('peanuts' was President Eisenhower's description of them), conveyed the urgency with which the Egyptian leader viewed their need to maintain both his standing at home and the national defence of Egypt. Eisenhower and his aides, while content to extend offers of economic help, had serious doubts about supplying weapons to Egypt. America had then a minimal military involvement in the

Opposite Egyptians bury one of the 39 soldiers killed at the military outpost in Gaza.

Left A British soldier displays some of the weapons found at Port Said during the crisis. After America's refusal to supply arms to Egypt, Nasser turned to Czechoslovakia.

Above Tradition and high-technology meet. The Aswan Dam project was finally completed in 1968 providing hydro-electric power for the surrounding industrial areas, as well as irrigation for formerly arid land.

region, and was by nature reluctant to increase the flow of armaments to any party in such volatile circumstances, quite apart from the severe disapproval from Britain and the pro–Israeli lobby at home which it might incur. Above all, there was a fundamental divergence between the supreme US policy of anti–Communism and Nasser's brand of neutralist, non–aligned nationalism. In the end, Nasser's warnings that he would seek arms elsewhere if necessary were dismissed as bluff, and Eisenhower made the fateful decision to stall indefinitely on Egypt's requests.

But Nasser was not bluffing. In September 1955 he announced that Egypt had signed a deal to buy large quantities of Soviet arms via Czechoslovakia. The immediate and dramatic effect was to boost his popularity among Egyptians and the Arab races at large as the champion of independence from the domineering West, and to confirm him in the eyes of Britain, France, Israel and others as the devil they had always feared him to be. It also took the Middle East straight into the Cold War firing line, by introducing for the first time the direct involvement of the Soviet Union. After overcoming an earlier aversion to the forces of 'bourgeois nationalism', the USSR now eagerly grasped at a chance to exploit Arab alienation from the West to extend its own influence.

Aswan finance withdrawn

Anti-Nasser feeling in Europe, Israel and America mounted, and in July 1956 Britain and the US dealt Nasser a serious blow by withdrawing an earlier promise to help finance what was to have been the cornerstone of Egypt's ambitious development programme—a project to dam the Nile at Aswan in Upper Egypt and provide electricity for industry and water for irrigation. Characteristically, Nasser responded, virtually on the spot, by striking back a blow which, certainly for Britain, carried an equally devastating punch.

On 26 July, before a vast crowd and over the radio sets of an Arab world bristling with excited anticipation, he proclaimed that Egypt had found another way to pay for the dam—by nationalising the Suez Canal. Nasser's legendary oratory praised the lives of 120,000 Egyptians who died building the Canal and denounced as Western exploitation a system in which over 90 per cent of the revenue from an Egyptian national asset went into foreign pockets. His actions were flawlessly supported under international law. As he spoke, a wave of pride and nationalist fervour swept over Arabs everywhere. The offices and installations of the Suez Canal Company were quietly and peacefully taken over by Egyptians.

European reaction to nationalization

The reaction of Britain's Conservative Prime Minister, Anthony Eden, to the nationalization of the Canal was to call an emergency Cabinet meeting at which he thundered, 'The Egyptian has his thumb on our windpipe', and, 'I

26 July 1956: In response to the Anglo–America withdrawal of funds for the Aswan project, Nasser nationalized the Suez Canal to provide the necessary finance. Over 50,000 Egyptians met in Manchia Square, Alexandria to hear Nasser's 'nationalization' speech.

51

don't care whether it's legal or not ... He's not going to get away with it.' His aggressive mood was echoed by the press and most of the Labour Opposition. It was also matched by a condescending disbelief that Egyptians were competent enough to manage and operate the waterway. However, Eden was now deeply satisfied that an excuse had arisen to deal with Nasser once and for all. Some four months earlier, following Jordan's abrupt dismissal of the British commander of its national army, (which Eden irrationally ascribed to Nasser's anti-British malice) the Prime Minister had shouted at one of his aides, 'But what's all this nonsense about isolating Nasser or "neutralising" him, as you call it? I want him destroyed, can't you understand?' (Evidence has emerged recently that British intelligence agencies did draw up plans to assassinate Nasser in the mid-1950s.) In fact Eden's temperament had become unbalanced by ill-health; as the Suez crisis ground on towards its climax his judgement was increasingly clouded by stress and fatigue.

August 1956: Prime Minister Anthony Eden during a television broadcast on the Suez crisis.

The violence of the British reaction to nationalization was paralleled in France, and both countries immediately agreed to have their military commands draw up plans for a joint invasion of Egypt. Nasser had rightly calculated that any military response by Britain and France would need some time to prepare, during which he hoped to consolidate his position internationally. His opponents, however, were resolved to use this period of forced delay to demonstrate to the world that they had explored all peaceful avenues before implementing the military 'solution' which in reality they had decided on from the start. Maddeningly for Eden, Nasser refused to rise to the bait and offer any provocation for the use of force: despite the withdrawal by Britain and France of their workers from the Canal, and their withholding of all dues for its use by their ships, Egyptian technicians kept the waterway working for all vessels, the numbers of which even increased.

The US, while resolutely opposed to Anglo–French military intervention, was broadly sympathetic to the position of its European allies, appreciating the extent of their dependence on Middle Eastern oil imported through the Canal. Fearful of the consequences of the threatened war and even for world peace, the US energetically supported attempts to find a diplomatic solution, such as the London Conferences of the Suez Canal Users Group in August and September (boycotted

Sir Anthony Eden, addressing the Suez Canal Users Group. Conferences in London in August and September 1956 failed to initiate a peaceful solution to the Suez question.

British military activity in Malta and Cyprus increased in the months leading up to the crisis. Helicopters, relatively new in the field of combat, played an important part for the Royal Marines.

6 November: A British centurion tank disembarks at Port Said.

by Egypt as being arranged against Egyptian interests). But as these moves, and the UN Security Council talks in early October, all foundered, and the Anglo–French military build-up in the Mediterranean continued, the US Administration became increasingly convinced that Britain and France were not negotiating in good faith: far from pursuing a solution, they were actively seeking war. Trans-Atlantic mistrust grew on both sides, as the European allies, angry that America would not support their course of action, began deliberately to withhold information, and even to mislead the US about their true plans.

Within days of the nationalization declaration, the French

Defence Minister had discussed with Israeli leaders the possibility of exploiting the anti-Nasser climate for a joint attack on Egypt. In early October, in blatant contravention of the Tripartite Declaration, France delivered 75 of its latest Mystere fighter planes to Israel. A few days later, a French minister and a general visited London secretly to ask Prime Minister Eden what Britain's reaction would be if Egypt were to be attacked by Israel. Eden was fascinated by the idea, and the Anglo–French Israeli conspiracy was sealed at another secret meeting between David Ben Gurion and the foreign ministers of Britain and France at Sèvres, France on 24 October. Five days later Israel attacked.

General Moshe Dayan details Israel's strategy at a Press Conference after the crisis.

6
Whose loss?

In human terms, Britain and France paid a surprisingly light price for the Suez war: out of the combined force of 22,000 men they sent to invade Egypt, 16 British soldiers were killed and 96 wounded; France lost 10, with 33 wounded. Israel's casualties were higher, some 200 killed and 900 wounded. No accurate count was ever made of Egypt's war dead and injured, but 1,000 soldiers are estimated to have

Fearing that the Israeli advance might trap them in the Sinai peninsula, Egyptian soldiers quickly withdrew from the area. In the chaos, many soldiers were lost in the desert, some dying of thirst. **Right** *An Israeli soldier finds heavy clothing discarded by the Egyptian soldiers.*

died in the Israeli bombing of Sinai, in addition to 4,000 wounded and 6,000 captured. As many as 1,000 died during the frantic scramble to pull the Egyptian army out of the peninsula before the Anglo–French attack was launched. In the chaos large numbers of soldiers were lost in the desert and perished of thirst and hunger. These heavy losses were the result principally of Israel's total control of the air, which it exploited mercilessly. At least another 1,000 died at Port Said, most of them, including many civilians, in the intense bombardment that preceded the Anglo–French landings.

Two young children sit in the ruins of their bombed home. In human terms, the Egyptians suffered the greatest losses during the Suez War.

Materially, however, despite the devastation of Port Said and the systematic destruction of roads, buildings and installations by the Israelis in Sinai, it was Britain and France, not Egypt, that were the real losers. From the Canal downwards, every British and French-owned asset was seized by the Egyptian state, on top of which Britain suffered a war-induced economic crisis that led to the re-introduction of something the British people thought they had finally seen the end of: rationing. And morally, Britain and France seemed overnight to have shed their highly-renowned international reputations with such a shabby, cynical conspiracy, involving as it did the blatant violation of the Charter of the United Nations, of which the two countries were permanent members of the Security Council, and of the Tripartite Declaration. The disillusionment of many was enhanced by the inevitable moral comparisons between the affair and the simultaneous Soviet invasion of Hungary.

Britain and France face international isolation

Politically, the cost was staggering. Britain and France had naively presumed that their assault on Egypt would induce the country's people to rise up against Nasser. Instead the result was that Nasser's personal popularity grew with the

Opposite November 1956: Damage caused by Anglo–French shell-fire in Port Said.

Below October 1956: Soviet tanks reach Budapest during the Hungarian uprising. Inevitably, moral comparisons were drawn between the Anglo–French–Israeli attack on Egypt and the Soviet intervention in Hungary.

1964: A general view of the Arab League headquarters in Cairo. In response to the Suez crisis, the Arab League pledged to assist Nasser in any future conflict.

wave of anti-Western reaction. British and French property was attacked in different areas of the Arab world, and Arab governments broke off relations with London and Paris. Syria blew up vital oil pipelines on its territory owned by an Anglo–French–American consortium. The Arab League pledged to join Nasser in any future fighting. And, of course, the Suez crisis boosted Arab resentment of Israel which was seen as an instrument of Western imperialism.

Great damage was also done to trans-Atlantic relations. The US administration was outraged by the way it had been deceived over British and French intentions, and deeply alarmed by the potentially explosive consequences of the Anglo–French intervention. Its mistrust and anger were reciprocated by Britain and France, who felt betrayed by America's refusal to back them fully in their anti-Nasser crusade. Nor was it just a case of a rift with the Americans: the international isolation of France and Britain over Suez was near total, as typefied by the 64–5 vote against them in the UN General Assembly at the height of the crisis. The British and French governments were also discredited at home. In May 1957 the French government fell, and the Fourth Republic collapsed the next year. In Britain too, the credibility of Eden's government, from which a number of senior figures resigned in protest during the crisis, had been too heavily undermined for it to survive long.

Naturally, the Suez crisis boosted Arab resentment of Israel. **Below** *Arabs demonstrate in Gaza, carrying an effigy of Israeli Prime Minister David Ben Gurion.*

Apart from the self-inflicted wounds to national prestige, to the economy and interests abroad, the government's claim that it had not colluded with Israel to attack Egypt (a charge never officially admitted to this day) was neither believable nor believed. Eden resigned, a sick man, on 9 January 1957, after less than two years in office. On his death in 1977, *The Times* called him 'the last Prime Minister to believe Britain was a great power and the first to confront a crisis which proved she was not'.

Among the conspirators, Israel alone emerged with any gains from the war. Its ships could now use the Gulf of Aqaba, and an international body, the United Nations Emergency Force (UNEF), was stationed in Sinai both to guard against any reimposition of the blockade and to act as a buffer between the Israeli and Egyptian armies. Israel's David Ben Gurion believed that Nasser had been taught a lesson.

January 1957: Arab refugees return to Sinai—a region safeguarded by the UNEF.

7
Suez: the aftermath

Looking back today, the Suez crisis was not just a culmi-
nation in Middle Eastern affairs but in the power structure
of the world as a whole. No other single incident demonstrated so conclusively that the era of the European
empires, which between them had once reigned supreme
over most of the surface of the globe, had finally drawn
to a close. The rude shattering of the myth of European
might and grandeur heralded the dawn of the superpower
age, as the struggle between East and West supplanted
the old contenders for world domination.

In Britain especially, people experienced new divisions
and confusion over the actions of their government in 1956,
and many controversies were aired for the first time about
the circumstances in which a nation had the right to employ
armed force, and the degree of democratic control over such
a process—arguments made familiar again in recent times
as a result of the 1982 Falklands war.

For the Arab world, the humiliation of Britain and France
in 1956 was the triumph of Arab nationalism, in a way
that irrevocably confirmed the West in Arab minds as a
mortal threat to their national interests and independence.

Soviet involvement in the Middle East
Suez ensured that anti-Western policies became an abiding
feature of the Middle East scene, to the extent that Arab
leaders came to risk assassination for failing to embrace such
policies at least outwardly. The pro-Western regime in Iraq
was toppled in 1958, and other Arab countries, most notably
Syria and Libya, soon followed Nasser's example and turned
to the Soviet bloc for arms. The Suez invasion thus achieved
the very opposite of its underlying rationale: to prevent Soviet
penetration of the region. Instead, it brought about the first
direct Soviet involvement in the Middle East, and has introduced the very real possibility that the Arabs and the Israelis

For the Arab world, the Anglo–French withdrawal from Egypt was a triumph for Arab 'nationalism'. Instead of discrediting Nasser, the Anglo–French attack had made him a hero.

An Egyptian commando unit equipped with Soviet arms.

may entangle the superpowers in direct confrontation with each other.

The seeds of the Arab–Israeli conflict were sown in Palestine long before the Suez crisis, but the latter nourished them and, with hindsight, made further wars inevitable. Egypt's 'victory' over France and Britain—in Arab eyes the heroic struggle of one poor, undeveloped nation against the combined forces of a regional superpower and two world powers—stoked the fires of Arab nationalism to dangerous levels. The leaders of the young Arab states, even realists like Nasser, were helpless to resist this tide of popular expectation and demand, swelled by boastful rhetoric, that soon the Arabs would march

irresistibly on to liberate Palestine.

In Israeli eyes, the 1956 invasion of Egypt demonstrated Israel's matchless military superiority over the biggest and best-equipped Arab army, and unleashed a confident agressiveness to rival that of the Arabs. For although Israel had achieved its goal of breaking the Egyptian blockade of the Gulf of Aqaba, it had also been forced to withdraw from the Sinai peninsula, the permanent addition of which to its territory it had firmly believed would be the principal reward of its efforts. Moreover, far from destroying the menace it perceived in Nasser, the Egyptian leader's prestige and influence were catapulted to record levels. Thus the Suez affair was

A British soldier rounds up some young Egyptians during the crisis. A growing nationalist pride led many Arab civilians to fight.

67

quickly established in Israeli minds as just a satisfactory dress rehearsal for the real battle.

This was not long in coming. In 1967 full-scale war again erupted between Israel and the Arab states, in which the latter were once more heavily defeated in a lightning campaign. A second Palestinian exodus ensued. Israel re-occupied the Sinai peninsula and also seized the last remaining areas of

Israeli commandos preparing for attack. In 1967 another war erupted between Israel and the Arab states, again over the issue of Palestine.

Palestine still under Arab control, the West Bank and Gaza Strip, since incorporated into Israel in all but name by a process of intensive Jewish settlement.

Sadat fights back
Sinai was to be fought over yet again, in October 1973, when a surprise assault across the Canal masterminded by Nasser's

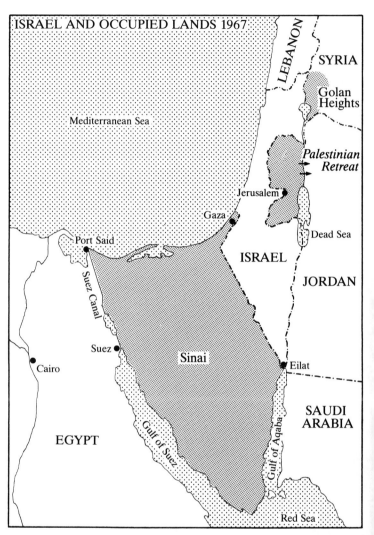

ISRAEL AND OCCUPIED LANDS 1967

LEBANON
SYRIA
Golan Heights
Mediterranean Sea
Palestinian Retreat
Jerusalem
Gaza
Dead Sea
ISRAEL
JORDAN
Port Said
Suez Canal
Suez
Sinai
Eilat
Cairo
Gulf of Suez
Gulf of Aqaba
SAUDI ARABIA
EGYPT
Red Sea

The shaded area shows the additional territory seized by Israel during the 1967 war. The occupation of these regions was declared illegal by the United Nations Resolution 242, as it was acquired by warfare, rather than by negotiation.

successor, President Anwar Sadat, smashed the myth of Israeli invincibility. The 1973 war achieved its limited aim of earning Egypt the right to meet Israel on almost equal terms; the outcome was the American-sponsored peace treaty between Israel and Egypt agreed at the US presidential retreat of Camp David in March 1979. Under this treaty the desert peninsula was restored to Egyptian sovereignty in April, 1982. But the issue of the dispossessed Palestinians, apparently consigned permanently to foreign exile or Israeli military occupation, remains as explosive as ever, and still constitutes arguably the single greatest threat to world peace. President Sadat,

70

architect of the first Arab–Israeli peace agreement, paid the price of Egypt's 'defection' to the West with his assassination in 1981, since when Camp David has increasingly assumed the character of a cold formality.

France and Britain have today by no means escaped or outlived the effects of the hatred sowed in Palestine, Egypt and Algeria (in particular), but it is the US, by virtue of its special relationship with Israel, which now bears the brunt of the Arab and Muslim animosity toward the West. Because of this, there is an irony and a sense of lost opportunity in looking back today on the Suez crisis, when America's standing in the Middle East was at its highest, characterised by attitudes of even-handedness toward the Arab–Israeli dispute and of opposition to the old colonialist and imperialist policies of the European powers. But Arab goodwill has long since been

March 1979: Egyptian President Anwar Sadat, American President Jimmy Carter and Israeli Prime Minister Menachem Begin clasp hands together outside the White House after the signing of the Camp David Peace Treaty. Sadly, their optimism was short-lived.

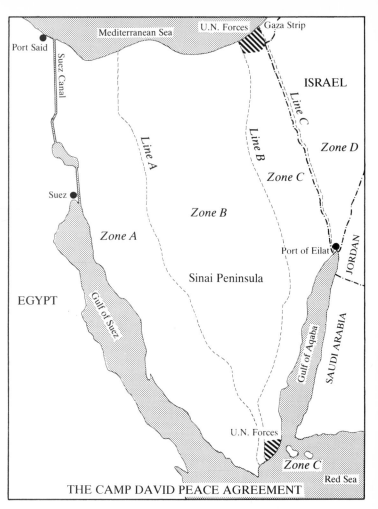

The terms of the Camp David Peace Treaty demanded the withdrawal of Israeli forces from the Sinai peninsula in three annual phases (as indicated on the map). In April 1982, Egypt did regain Sinai.

THE CAMP DAVID PEACE AGREEMENT

transformed into antagonism as America's Middle East policies have become increasingly narrow minded—with the unquestioning military, economic and moral support for Israel and the global fight against Communism. Policies which obscure the regional factors at the root of the conflict. Most important among these is the need for Israel and the Palestinians to agree on a formula for peaceful co-existence. For this reason especially, President Eisenhower's words in the aftermath of the Suez war are as appropriate today as then:

'Should a nation which attacks and occupies foreign territory in the face of United Nations disapproval be allowed to impose conditions on its withdrawal? If we agree that armed attack can properly achieve the purpose of the assailant, then I fear we will have turned back the clock of international order ... If the United Nations once admits that international disputes can be settled by using force, then we will have destroyed the very foundation of the organization and the best hope of establishing a world order. That would be a disaster for us all ...'

October 1981: A man in Egyptian army uniform assassinates President Sadat at pointblank range.

Glossary

Allies The countries who fought against the Axis powers (see below) and Japan during the Second World War (Britain, the Commonwealth countries, USA, USSR, France and Poland).

Arab Conquests The expansion in the seventh century AD of the Arab tribes from their common homeland of the Arabian peninsula (what is today Saudi Arabia). After the death of the Prophet Muhammad in AD 632, the Arabs embarked on a series of rapid military conquests—resulting today in an Arab world stretching from the Atlantic in the west to the Persian Gulf in the east.

Anarchy General lawlessness and the lack of government in a society.

Axis Powers The alliance of Nazi Germany, Fascist Italy and Japan, established in 1936 and lasting until defeat in the Second World War.

Baghdad Pact Signed in February 1955, first between Iraq and Turkey, then later Britain, Iran and Pakistan. The Baghdad Pact was a British-sponsored alliance whose aim was to recruit Middle East countries into the pro–West, anti–Soviet camp. The pact was vigorously opposed by Nasser and other Arab nationalists as a plot to perpetuate the influence of Western imperialism in the region.

Collusion A fraudulent undertaking, made in secret.

'Eastern Question' The 19th Century struggle of the European powers for influence over the territories of the decaying Ottoman Empire. The statesmen of the day in France and Britain approached the issue in terms of protecting the Christian minorities within the Empire and of preventing Russian expansionism through Turkey into the Mediterranean.

FLN (National Liberation Front): The Algerian popular movement for independence from French colonial rule. Its guerillas fought French forces in Algeria during the rebellion from 1956 until 1962, when Algeria became independent.

Free Officers Movement Underground organisation

founded by Nasser and fellow Egyptian army officers after the Second World War, with the aim of overthrowing the government and expelling the British from the country. The movement seized power in Egypt in a coup in 1952.

Imperialism   The policy or practice of extending a state's rule over other territories.

Isthmus   A narrow strip of land connecting two relatively large land areas.

Khedive   A special title conferred on the rulers of Egypt by the Sultan of the Ottoman Empire in 1867. Although in theory Egypt was part of the Empire, and its rulers thus only provincial governors, in practice powerful Egyptian rulers like Muhammad Ali and his descendants were completely independent of the Sultan.

League of Nations   The forerunner of the present day United Nations, the League of Nations formally came into being in 1920 with the primary intention of preventing further world wars. Its role as arbiter in international disputes collapsed with the polarisation of nations prior to the Second World War.

Mandate   The system of Mandates was set up by the League of Nations (see above), giving countries an internationally recognised authority (or mandate) to administer colonial territories with the aim eventually of preparing them for self–government and independence. On the collapse of the Ottoman Empire after the First World War, France and Britain were awarded Mandates over many of the Arab territories they had occupied during the war against Turkey.

Muslim Brotherhood   An underground Islamic movement founded in Egypt in the 1920s, which turned increasingly to military and terrorist activities to achieve its goals. Though suppressed by Nasser in the 1950s, it has since flourished and spread to other Muslim countries.

Non-alignment   A country's policy not to be part of a major alliance or power bloc.

Ottoman Empire   The Turkish Empire ruled by the dynasty of Ottoman sultans from Constantinople (modern day Istanbul) and extending from eastern Europe over most of the Arab world. It lasted 400 years, from 1517 until the end of the First World War in 1918.

Protectorate   A territory largely controlled by, but not annexed to, a stronger state.

Superpower An extremely powerful nation. The USSR and the USA are often referred to as superpowers.

Tripartite Declaration The agreement signed in 1950 by the three main Western powers, the United States, Britain and France, following on the first Arab–Israeli war of 1948–9. In it all three powers pledged themselves to action, within or without the framework of the United Nations, to resist any attempt by either Israel or the Arabs to change the 1949 armistice lines by force of arms.

Ultimatum A final proposal in a time of crisis.

Wafd The first formally organised group to represent the Egyptian nationalists, the Wafd was formed in 1919 as a delegation sent abroad to put the case internationally for Egypt's independence. The Wafd Party dominated the early years of Egypt's constitutional parliament, and remains an active contender for power today.

Veto The power to prevent actions proposed by others.

Zionism The Jewish political movement to establish a national home for the Jews in Palestine. Zionism's basic goal was realised with the establishment of the State of Israel in 1948.

Further reading

HARPER, P *The Arab–Israeli Issue* (Wayland, 1986)

HIRST, D *The Gun and the Olive Branch* (Futura, 1984)

LOVE, K *Suez: The Twice Fought War* (Longman, 1970)

MANSFIELD, P *The Arabs* (Penguin, 1980)

NEFF, D *Warriors at Suez* (The Linden Press / Simon & Schuster, 1981)

NUTTING, A *No end of a Lesson: The Story of Suez* (Constable & Co, 1967)

Index

Picture acknowledgements

The publishers would like to thank the following for allowing their photographs to be reproduced in this book: Associated Press 15, 32, 38, 40, 41, 42, 43, 44 (both), 46, 48, 55, 56, 57, 60, 61, 62, 71, 73; BBC Hulton Picture Library 13, 14, 19, 21, 37, 47, 52, 53, 67; Camera Press 18; Imperial War Museum 12, 17 (both), 24 (top), 31, 33, 34, 54 (both); John Hillelson 59; Middle East Centre, Oxford (Blyth Collection) 28; Popperfoto *cover*, *frontispiece*, 10, 11 (top), 16, 50–51, 65; R. Cecil Rhodes (Hawkins Collection) 24–25; TOPHAM 11 (bottom), 23, 27, 29, 30 (both), 39, 58, 66, 68–69. The maps on pages 9, 20, 22, 26, 36, 70 and 72 by Malcolm S. Walker.